HIS MIGHTY HAND

A Vision of Prayer

by Lou Bardal

illustrated by Elsa Hammond

Copyright © 2015 by Lou Bardal

His Mighty Hand
A Vision of Prayer
by Lou Bardal
illustrated by Elsa Hammond

Printed in the United States of America

Edited by Xulon Press

ISBN 9781498453547

All rights reserved solely by the author. The author guarantees all contents are original and do not infringe upon the legal rights of any other person or work. No part of this book may be reproduced in any form without the permission of the author. The views expressed in this book are not necessarily those of the publisher.

Scripture quotations taken from the Amplified Bible (AMP). Copyright © 1954, 1958, 1962, 1964, 1965, 1987 by The Lockman Foundation. Used by permission. All rights reserved.

Scripture quotations taken from the New King James Version (NKJV). Copyright © 1979, 1980, 1982 by Thomas Nelson, Inc. Used by permission. All rights reserved.

Scripture quotations taken from the New International Version (NIV). Copyright © 1973, 1978, 1984, 2011 by Biblica, Inc.™. Used by permission. All rights reserved.

Scripture quotations taken from the English Standard Version (ESV). Copyright © 2001 by Crossway, a publishing ministry of Good News Publishers. Used by permission. All rights reserved.

Scripture quotations taken from the New American Standard Bible (NASB). Copyright © 1960, 1962, 1963, 1968, 1971, 1972, 1973, 1975, 1977, 1995 by The Lockman Foundation. Used by permission. All rights reserved.

www.xulonpress.com

Dedication

This book is dedicated to my Lord and Savior, Jesus Christ, to my husband, Dave, my son Michael and his wife, Priya, my son Todd and his wife, Cassia, and my grandchildren, Mira, Elijah, Isaac, Noah, Charlie, and Lily.

Acknowledgements

I would like to thank Mark Virkler for teaching me the four keys to hearing God's voice. I would also like to thank Elsa Hammond for her beautiful illustrations used in this book.

One day I met with Jesus in a vision on the sandy beach beside the Sea of Galilee.

I was so happy to be with Jesus, and He was so happy to be with me.

Jesus and I walked along the beach holding hands. He told me how glad He was to be with me. We laughed together as we walked.

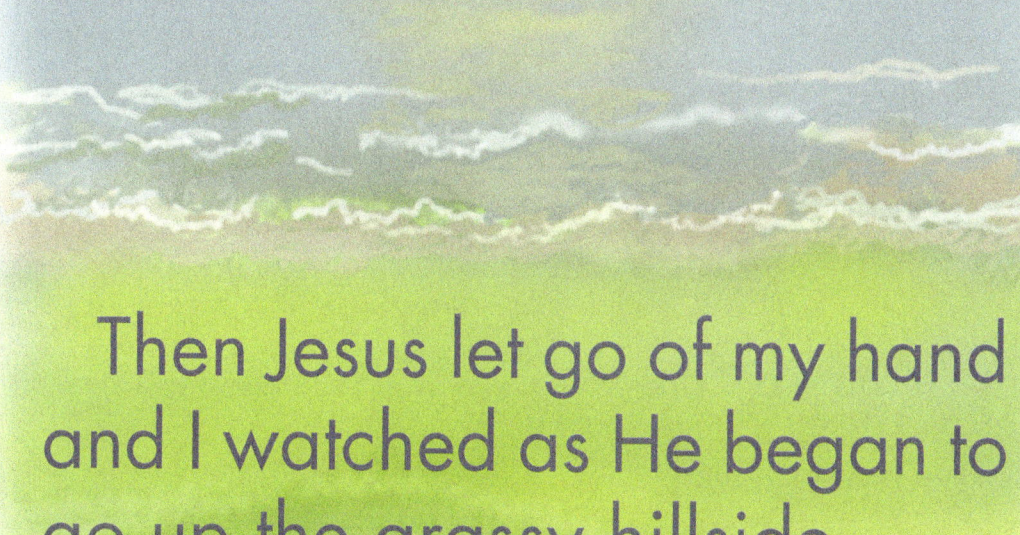

Then Jesus let go of my hand and I watched as He began to go up the grassy hillside.

I followed Him and He went a little way ahead of me and sat down on a big, brown rock.

As I looked up at Him, He lowered His hand all the way to the ground, just in front of my feet. But His hand was very, very large and I was very, very tiny.

He said, "Step onto My hand."

But I just stood there and began to cry.

"Why are you crying?" Jesus gently asked.

"Because I am so afraid. Your hand is so very big and I am so, so tiny," I answered.

"Oh, do not be afraid," He kindly answered. "I am here! I am God! I am love Himself and there is no fear in love."

So I stepped onto His big hand and even though I was so tiny, He lifted me up to God.

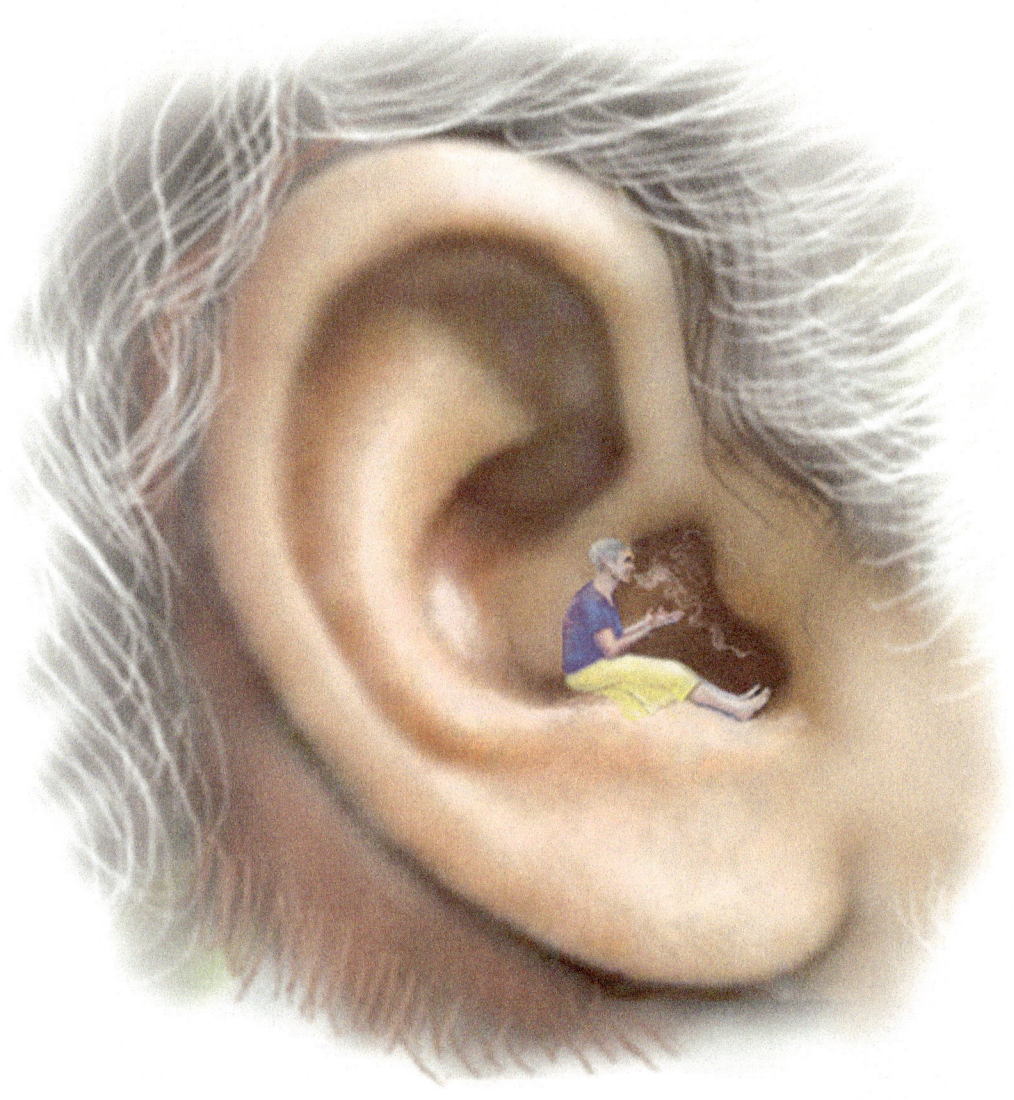

Next He set me down on that "little shelf" just inside God's big ear, and I began to pray in the words of the Holy Spirit.

Suddenly, God lifted me out of His ear and brought me around to His mouth.

There was a great big waterfall flowing out of God's mouth. I saw many people, children and adults going down the waterfall. They were laughing and splashing and enjoying the water.

"Would you like to go down the waterfall, too?" He asked.

"Yes! Please let me join them," I answered.

So God placed me into the wonderful, refreshing water.

I began to laugh and twirl around in the water. Suddenly I realized that everyone in my family was floating down the waterfall right behind me! We were all enjoying splashing in the mighty living water of God!

Part Two
Story of the Vision

The following is the story of how I received the vision as told in this book and the scriptures that support what I saw in this vision.

I had watched Mark Virkler's video, "A Stroll along the Sea of Galilee" with the narration and music done by Julie True. I imagined myself walking with Jesus on the path near the Sea of Galilee. I wrote down the question I would ask Him beforehand. The question was "What do You want to say to me, Lord?"

I purposely imagined myself walking with Jesus along the path. I noticed the green hills and the lake. It was a warm sunny day. Then we walked down next to the lake in the sand, but at this point, the Holy Spirit "took over" and the scene that I was imagining became a vision.

At this point I saw Jesus walk up the hillside to a large rock. He sat down and asked me to come too. I just stood there and the next thing I saw was His hand reaching down to me. However, His hand had become a giant hand and He put it on the ground right in front of my feet and invited me to step onto it. But I was too afraid to take the step.

I was afraid to step onto His hand because I was so afraid of having a vision. I had been taught that I could see Jesus in vision back in 1987 and I had seen two visions of Him. However, shortly after that I read a book by a Christian author who stated that to visualize Jesus was a New Age practice. I had become so frightened after reading the book that I threw it away, but the seeds of doubt remained. I had long since stopped asking Jesus what He was doing and had not "looked" to see Him in a vision.

However in 2009 I purchased Mark Virkler's cd's and dvd's titled, "How to Hear God's Voice" and began to pursue hearing God's voice again. Mark teaches that there are four keys to hearing God's voice. They are: "Be still, fix your eyes on Jesus (or use vision); tune to spontaneous thoughts and pictures and journal these thoughts." I had journaled quite extensively for the next three years, but I had not practiced using vision very much.

When I saw Jesus lower His hand down to my feet I began to cry. In fact, I wept profusely. If someone had been in the house they would have heard me crying. I then admitted to the Lord that I was afraid to step onto His hand. I wept and wept for quite a while and then my weeping changed into hysterical laughter. It was the joyful holy laughter that I have experienced before. It was so wonderful I wanted to share it with someone so I called a friend, who had also experienced this same holy laughter with me several times before. She did not receive the holy laughter at that time and after I had calmed down, we talked for a while and then I got off of the phone.

I felt brave after I hung up the phone, so I went back to the vision where I had left off before the phone call. In the vision I stepped onto the hand of Jesus. As I did this, I began to laugh again and I heard the Lord say, "Who is he who will condemn you? Will Christ Jesus, Who died for you?"

When I stepped onto His hand I saw myself being lifted up by His huge hand. Jesus looked like a giant! Yet I was very, very small on His hand. As He lifted me up He held me so gently and delicately like someone might hold a butterfly. I was as tiny as a seed. Next, I saw Him place me right inside the huge ear of God. In fact He sat me down on that outer area of his ear and it was as though I was sitting on a bench.

My thoughts were, "You are great and mighty! I am so very tiny, but You place me right into your ear. It is like a bench because Your ear is so huge."

I sat there speaking to Him; I was praying in the spirit. Then I mentioned the two people I had prayed with the day before at church. I told the Lord that I wanted them to "get it" and be healed! Then I heard Him say, "You heal them Lou, just like I healed people when I walked the earth. You don't heal them in your name, Lou, you heal them in My name."

Next I saw the Lord take me from His ear and bring me around to His mouth and I began to laugh again. Then I saw a great river of water flowing out of God's mouth. It looked like a waterfall. I saw people floating down the waterfall. They were laughing and splashing each other as they went down the waterfall. Then the Lord asked me if I would like to join them. I said, "Yes!" So He placed me on the waterfall coming out of His mouth. There were millions of other people who were in this River of water flowing out of the mouth of God! We were all laughing and rejoicing! "HA, HA, HA-ing—HA-llelujah--HA-llelujahing!"

Then the Lord said to me, "Yes, you are in the spirit when you pray in tongues! Yes! Yes! I am the Mighty Great Big King. Although you seem small to yourself you are very precious to Me. I move you by My Mighty Hand and sit you in My ear and your tiny mouth reverberates with My words," says the Lord. "It is My mighty word that you speak and My words in your mouth release the angels. Yes! My words are creative words of power and life and of the Spirit and My words accomplish what I intend them to accomplish. I have given you a gift--the gift of speaking in tongues and these words proceed from my mouth and My Spirit and they carry My desires and purposes! They shall accomplish the things that I desire for I watch over My words to accomplish them!"

Scripture References to Support Vision

Next I looked down at my Bible, which was in my lap and I read these words, "Incline your ear, submit and consent to the divine will and come to Me; hear and your soul will revive and I will make an everlasting covenant or league with you, even the sure mercy, kindness, goodwill and compassion promised to David (Isaiah 55:3 AMP).

Then I looked at verses 2, 12, and 13:

> Why do you spend your money for that which is not bread, and your earnings for what does not satisfy? Hearken diligently to Me, and eat what is good, and let your soul delight itself in fatness (the profuseness of spiritual joy)... (and verses 12 and 13) For you shall go out from the spiritual exile caused by sin and evil into the homeland with joy and be led forth by your Leader, the Lord Himself, and His word with peace; the mountains and the hills shall break forth before you into singing, and all the trees of the field shall clap their hands. Instead of the thorn (the curse) shall come up the cypress tree, and instead of the brier shall come up the myrtle tree; and it shall be to the Lord for a name of renown, for an everlasting sign of jubilant exaltation and memorial to His praise, which shall not be cut off.

These verses speak of "delight," "profuseness of spiritual joy" and "jubilant exaltation." In this vision with the Lord I certainly experienced these feelings expressed by my laughter.

James 4:10 (AMP) came to mind after seeing this vision. "Humble yourselves (feeling very insignificant) in the presence of the Lord, and He will exalt you (He will make your lives significant)."

In the vision, I was very, very tiny in comparison to the Lord's hand.

1 Peter 5:6 says, "Humble yourselves therefore under the mighty hand of God, that he might exalt you in due time: Casting all your care upon him; for he cares for you." The hand of Jesus became the mighty hand of God. When I finally stepped onto His hand I was truly casting all my cares on Him, for I was placing my whole self into His hand!

Another verse that brings out this thought is found in Acts 16:30 and 31 in the Amplified Bible. In this passage of scripture the jailer in this story asks Paul and Silas:

Men what must I do that I may be saved? And they answered, 'Believe in the Lord Jesus Christ (give yourself up to Him, take yourself out of your own keeping and entrust yourself into His keeping) and you will be saved, (and this applies both to) you and to your household as well.'

In the days that followed this vision I noticed a lot of verses to confirm it. "He raises the poor out of the dust and lifts the needy out of the ash heap, that He may seat him with princes—with the princes of His people" (Psalm 113:5-8, AMP).

The Prince of Peace placed me into the very ear of God.

Why should the nations say, Where is now their God? But our God is in heaven; He does whatever he pleases. The idols of the nations are silver and gold, the work of men's hands. They have mouths, but they speak not; eyes have they, but they see not; they have ears, but they hear not; noses they have, but they smell not; they have hands, but they handle not; feet have they, but they walk not; neither can they make a sound with their throats. They who make idols are like them; so are all who trust in and lean on them. Oh Israel, trust and take refuge in the Lord...He is their help and their shield (Psalm 115:2-9 AMP).

I saw that the Living God is not like idols! He has eyes that see, ears that hear, and hands that lift and a mouth that speaks!

I love the Lord, because He has heard my voice and my supplications. Because He has inclined His ear to me, therefore I will call upon Him as long as I live. The pains of death surrounded me and the pangs of Sheol laid hold of me; I found trouble and sorrow. Then I called upon the name of the Lord: 'Oh Lord, I implore you, deliver my soul!' Gracious is the Lord, and righteous; Yes, our God is merciful. The Lord preserves the simple; I was brought low, and He saved me. Return to your rest, O my soul, for the Lord has dealt bountifully with you. For You have delivered my soul from death, My eyes from tears, and my feet from falling. I will walk before the Lord in the land of the living (Psalms 116:1—9 NKJV).

The Lord turned my tears into laughter and delivered me from the fear of death, or of being separated from God because I had done a "new age" thing. He made Himself real to me!

"It is God Who sits above the circle of the earth, and <u>its inhabitants are like grasshoppers</u>; it is He Who stretches out the heavens like gauze curtains and spreads them out like a tent to dwell in" (Isaiah 40:22 AMP).

When I stepped onto the Lord's hand I was very very tiny, as small as a grasshopper.

The Lord is my Rock and my Fortress and my Deliverer; My God, my Rock, in Him will I take refuge; my Shield and the Horn of my salvation; my Stronghold and my Refuge, my Savior—You save me from violence. I call on the Lord, Who is worthy to be praised, and I am saved from my enemies. For the waves of death enveloped me, the torrents of <u>destruction made me afraid.</u> The cords of Sheol were entangling me; I encountered the snares of death. In my distress I called upon the Lord; I cried to my God, and he heard my voice from His temple; <u>my cry came into His ears</u> (2 Samuel 22:2-7 AMP).

I was afraid of vision because of the things I had read in a book.

Jesus has delivered us from the ultimate fear, the fear of death, which is the fear that we can be separated from God if we do something God does not approve of; and He placed me into the very ear of God the Father:

> He delivered me from my strong enemy, from those who hated me, for they were too mighty for me. They came upon me in the day of my calamity, but the Lord was my stay. He brought me forth into a large place; He delivered me because He delighted in me...He makes my feet like the hinds' (firm and able); He sets me secure and confident upon the heights (2 Samuel 22:18-20, 34 AMP).

I stepped onto the Lord's giant hand and He lifted me up on His hand! He lifted me up to God's ear and set me down inside it. What height could be more secure and confident?

Jesus said,

> And I give unto them eternal life; and they shall never perish, neither shall any *man* pluck them out of my hand. My Father, which gave them to me is greater than all; and *no man* is able to pluck them out of my Father's hand (John 10:28—29 KJV).

And: "You give me Your shield of victory; you stoop down to make me great" (2 Samuel 22:36, NIV).

Philippians 2:6-11 AMP describes Jesus;

> Who being essentially one with God and in the form of God...did not think this equality with God a thing to be eagerly grasped or retained, but stripped Himself of all privileges as to assume the guise of a servant in that

He became like men and was born a human being. And after He had appeared in human form, He abased and humbled Himself (still further) and carried His obedience to the extreme of death even the death of the cross! Therefore (<u>because He stooped so low</u>) God has highly exalted Him and has freely bestowed on Him the name that is above every name, that in (at) the name of Jesus every knee should (must) bow, in heaven and earth, and every tongue confess and acknowledge that Jesus Christ is Lord, to the glory of God the Father.

Jesus sat on the rock and reached His hand down—He stooped down—to my very feet to lift me up!

But God—so rich is He in His mercy! Because of and in order to satisfy the great and wonderful and intense love with which He loved us, even when we were dead and slain by our own shortcomings and trespasses, He made us alive together in fellowship and in union with Christ... and He raised us up together with Him and made us sit down together (giving us joint seating with Him) in the heavenly sphere (by virtue of our being) in Christ Jesus (Ephesians 2:4-5 AMP).

And He has given us His very Name to use!

And I will do (I Myself will grant) whatever you ask in My Name (as presenting all that I AM), so that the Father may be glorified and extolled in (through) the Son! Yes I will grant (I Myself will do for you) whatever you shall ask in My Name (as presenting all that I AM) (John 14:13-14 AMP).

Jesus placed me in the very ear of the Father! In John 11:42, Jesus said, "Father, I thank You that You have heard me. Yes, I know You always hear and listen to Me." Obviously, if we have been raised up together with Him and made to sit down together with Him in heavenly places, God hears us, too!

1 John 5:14 AMP says:

> And this is the confidence (the assurance, the privilege of boldness) which we have in Him: (we are sure) that if we ask anything (make any request) according to His will (in agreement with His own plan), He listens to and hears us. And if (since) we (positively) know that He listens to us in whatever we ask, we also know (with settled and absolute knowledge) that we have (granted us as our present possessions) the requests made of Him.

My vision shows very clearly that God was listening to my prayer. I was praying in tongues, or in the spirit (see 1 Corinthians 14:14). I was praying the very will of God. John 16:13 AMP states,

> But when He, the Spirit of Truth (the Truth-giving Spirit) comes…He will not speak His own message (on His own authority); but He will tell whatever He hears from the Father; He will give the message that has been given to Him, and He will announce and declare to you the things that are to come (that will happen in the future).

And the things that will happen in the future are the plans of God that shall come to pass.

"His voice was like the sound of many waters" (Revelation 1:15).

I saw a giant waterfall coming out of God's mouth! That's His voice. Jesus said:

> He who believes in Me (who cleaves to and trusts in and relies on Me as the Scripture has said, From his innermost being shall flow (continuously) springs and rivers of living water. But He was speaking here of the Spirit, whom those who believed (trusted, had faith) in Him were afterward to receive (John 7:38-39 AMP).

When we pray in tongues we speak the words that the Holy Spirit gives us to utter, we are praying to God (see 1 Corinthians 14:2), and the words of the Spirit are the words of our Father, God (see John 16:12 and 13). Jesus said that out of the overflow of the heart the mouth speaks (see Matthew 12:34). The words that the Holy Spirit gives us to speak are the living water flowing out of our mouths. Our words are the same as the words of the Father and His words produce life! Hence the many people in the waterfall of God.

I shared my vision with a prayer partner and the next day she called me to share a scripture verse she had read that day in her Bible reading. She said that it reminded her of my vision. It was Psalm 31:5 KJV "Into thine hand I commit my spirit, thou hast redeemed me, O LORD God of truth."

The following verses seem to sum up the entire vision. For it is what Jesus did as a man, and then He became our High Priest. This verse is the epitome of prayer. This verse sums up Who Jesus is and thus tells us what it means to pray "in Jesus Name." Jesus prayed this way for us and as us!

> In the days of His flesh (Jesus) offered up definite, special petitions (for that which He not only wanted but needed) and supplications with strong crying and tears to Him Who was (always) able to save Him (out) from death, and He was heard because of His reverence toward God (His godly fear, His piety, in that He shrank from the horrors

of separation from the bright presence of the Father) (Hebrews 5:7 AMP).

And,

But now in Christ Jesus, you who once were (so) far away, through (by, in) the blood of Christ have been brought near. For He is (Himself) our peace...and He came and preached peace to you who were far off and peace to those who were near. For it is through Him that we both (whether far off or near) now have (access) by one (Holy) Spirit to the Father (so that we may approach Him) (Ephesians 2:13, 14, 17, 18 AMP).

Prayer for Salvation

After reading my story, you may be wondering, "Is this relationship with God and Jesus Christ possible for anyone?" Yes, it is! Anyone can come into a close personal relationship with God through Jesus Christ. The Bible says in Romans 10:9 and 10 AMP,

If you acknowledge and confess with your lips that Jesus is Lord and in your heart believe...that God raised Him from the dead, you will be saved. For with the heart a person believes...and so is justified (declared righteous, acceptable to God), and with the mouth He confesses (declares openly and speaks out freely his faith) and confirms his salvation.

God hears the prayers of the righteous, so if you want Him to hear your prayers you can pray the following prayer.
"I confess that Jesus Christ is Lord. I believe that Jesus Christ is the

Son of God. I believe that Jesus died on the cross for me and that His blood completely cleansed me of all sin. I believe God raised Him from the dead. I ask You, Oh God, to give me your precious gift of eternal life. I open my heart to You, Lord Jesus, come into my heart by your Spirit now and live in me. Thank you for loving me. Thank you for answering this prayer! Amen!"

If you prayed the above prayer, then you are now born from above. You are now a new creation in Christ Jesus. You can now get to know God, the Father, Jesus Christ, who is God, the Son, and God, the Holy Spirit. You were made righteous! Your spirit has been joined to the Lord and the Bible says, "He that is joined to the Lord is one spirit with Him" (1 Corinthians 6:17). The Spirit of the Son has taken up residence in your body. However your mind, which still thinks like it always has, needs to be renewed. How can this happen? How can you learn the thoughts of God?

God, who is a Spirit, has taken up residence in your very spirit and He wants to teach you all about His Son Jesus! So you need to be taught by the Holy Spirit. You must allow the Holy Spirit to teach you all things! So you might be thinking, "How do I allow the Holy Spirit to teach me all things?"

Jesus said, "But when He, the Spirit of Truth comes, He will guide you into all the Truth" (John 16:13). In other words He will explain everything about Jesus to you.

"How does He do that?" you might ask.

He speaks!

Here's the rest of the above verse that I started quoting.

> But when the Spirit of Truth comes, He will guide you into all the Truth (the whole, full Truth). For He will not speak His own message (on His own authority); but He will tell whatever He hears from the Father; He will give the message that has been given to Him, and He will

announce and declare to you the things that are to come (that will happen in the future) (John 16:13 AMP).

Jesus said that, "The Holy Spirit, Whom the Father will send in My Name (in My place, to represent Me and act on My behalf), will teach you all things" (see John 14:26 AMP).

Now you might be saying," I want the Holy Spirit to teach me all about Jesus. How can this happen since I am only a human being?"

Did you realize that this is just about the same thing Mary asked the angel, Gabriel, when he came and announced to her that she was going to have a baby and she would name him, Jesus? The angel told her, "He will be great and will be called the Son of the Most High. And the Lord God will give to him the throne of his father David and he will reign over the house of Jacob forever and of his kingdom there will be no end" (Luke 1:31—33 ESV).

Upon hearing this, Mary asked, "How shall this be, since I have no husband?" (Luke 1:34 ESV)

The angel, Gabriel, gave her this answer, "The Holy Spirit will come upon you, and the power of the Most High will overshadow you; therefore the child to be born will be called holy—the Son of God." (Luke 1:35 ESV).

And Mary answered, "Behold, I am the servant of the Lord, let it be to me according to your word" (Luke 1:38 ESV). (Please note; Mary would not have become pregnant with Jesus unless she had said this!)

Well, Jesus said the same thing to His disciples just before He ascended into Heaven before their very eyes! He commanded them that they should not depart from Jerusalem, but wait for the promise of the Father, "For John baptized with water, but you will be baptized with the Holy Spirit not many days from now" (Acts 1:5 ESV).

And here's what Jesus said that was almost word for word what the angel, Gabriel, said to Mary. Jesus said, ..."you will receive power, after that the Holy Spirit is come upon you; and you shall be witnesses unto me" (Acts 1:8 ESV).

So 120 of the disciples obeyed the command of Jesus and waited in Jerusalem for 10 days. They were saying by their actions, "Be it unto me according to Your word, Jesus." In Acts 2 we read what happened when the Holy Spirit came upon them with power. There was the sound like a mighty rushing wind, and there were tongues resembling fire that sat upon each of their heads and "they began to speak in other languages as the Holy Spirit kept giving them clear and loud expression…in appropriate words" (Acts 2:2-4 AMP).

There it is. The Holy Spirit spoke through them. They spoke the words that He gave them to speak. In Isaiah 28:11 AMP it says, "…the Lord will teach the rebels in a more humiliating way by men with stammering lips and another tongue will He speak to this people…and teach them His lessons."

You, too, can ask your heavenly Father to give you the Holy Spirit, and Jesus will baptize you in the Holy Spirit and power. Then you yield your tongue to the Holy Spirit and begin to speak out loud the "seemingly non-sensical" words that He gives you to speak. I say, "non-sensical" because that's how these words will sound to your mind! However, you can rest assured on the promise of Jesus that if you ask your Heavenly Father for the Holy Spirit you will not get a stone or a counterfeit. You will get real words! (See Luke 11:9—13)

If you will yield your tongue to the words the Holy Spirit gives you to speak and continue daily speaking these "seemingly non-sensical" words the Holy Spirit will teach you all things. (see 1 John 2:27) You will begin to know Jesus, your Heavenly Father, and the Holy Spirit in an intimate way. You will actually be sitting in the great big ear of your Heavenly Father too. As you read your Bible you can pray in this language of the Spirit and God's written word will begin to make sense to you. You will understand it! Why? Because Jesus promised that when the Holy Spirit comes He will guide and explain all the Truth to you!

Now, are you ready to ask the Father for the Holy Spirit? If you are then you can say something like this to God.

"Heavenly Father, I ask you for the promise of your Holy Spirit and power. Lord Jesus Christ, thank you that your blood has cleansed me from all sin. I ask you, Lord Jesus, to baptize me in your Holy Spirit and give me this new language of the Spirit."

Now begin to thank Jesus out loud! Just start saying, "Thank you Jesus! Thank you, Jesus! Thank you, Jesus!" Keep on saying, "Thank you, Jesus." But at some point don't say "thank you" in English, allow yourself to speak those syllables (that seem nonsensical) to come out of your mouth. You may feel stupid or even like a child. But remember, Jesus said, "Whoever does not receive the Kingdom of God like a child shall not enter it at all" (Luke 18:17 NAS).

As you speak those "seemingly nonsensical" syllables allow them to continue to flow out of your mouth. You are speaking the words of the Holy Spirit of God! Do not allow your mind to say, "Oh, this is nothing, this is nonsense." Your mind will try to say this to you because it does not understand what you are saying. But you must speak these words by faith. (A good definition of faith is, "Perceiving as real fact what is not revealed to the senses" Hebrews 11:1 AMP). You speak them in child like faith knowing that your Heavenly Father has said that He will give His Holy Spirit to those who ask. You simply believe what God has said in His Word. That is another definition of faith!

Another thing to know is that you can speak in this language of the Holy Spirit anytime you want, just like you can speak in English or your own native language anytime you want. You can choose to speak in this language of the Holy Spirit and God will be teaching you His lessons, as He promised in Isaiah 28. You will also be praying the mysteries unto God when you speak these words (see 1 Corinthians 14:2).

When you speak these words you are actually seated in the very ear of your Father God! (Just like I was!) Then you can ask for "the understanding" of these words and when you speak forth the words in your own language (like English), you will become part of the waterfall coming forth out of God's mouth! And others will enter this waterfall coming out of God's mouth! Just like in my vision!

Another thing to remember is that this gift of speaking in tongues is not just for a special few. Jesus said in Mark 16:16-17 AMP, "And these attesting signs will accompany those who believe; in My name…they will speak in new languages."

May God bless you in your new journey with your Guide, the Holy Spirit! And may you see yourself seated in the ear of God, and flowing in the water of the Spirit coming out of His mouth!

References

"A Stroll Along the Sea of Galilee", New life for Your Daily Devotions, copyright 2012 Mark and Pattie Virkler, Free Resources at: CWGMinistries.org

Music to Journal By, Words and music, Julie True, Length 30:00, P and Copyright 2012 TrueHeart Worship (BMI) available at: www.JulieTrue.com

DVD and CD series: Mark Virkler, "How to Hear God's Voice", Communion with God Ministries, www.cwgministries.org

CPSIA information can be obtained
at www.ICGtesting.com
Printed in the USA
LVOW02s1023181115
463039LV00003B/3/P